FLORENCE

FROM THE AIR

This book is dedicated to
Gisella, to Lucia and to all Florentines.

Endpapers: *Golden dusk on the Arno. Light*
effects worthy of an impressionist painting.
Pages 4-5: *Rowing race on the Arno.*

Florence From the Air
Translated by J. Tyler Tuttle
© **Editions Didier Millet/les Nouvelles Editions du Pacifique** 1989
23 avenue Villemain, 75014 Paris
First published in Great Britain in 1990 by
George Weidenfeld & Nicolson Limited
91 Clapham High Street, London SW4 7TA
ISBN 0 297 83010 4

Printed by Arti Grafiche Amilcare Pizzi S.P.A., Italie

FLORENCE
FROM THE AIR

TEXT BY MARIO SABBIETI / PHOTOGRAPHS BY GUIDO ALBERTO ROSSI

Weidenfeld & Nicolson
London

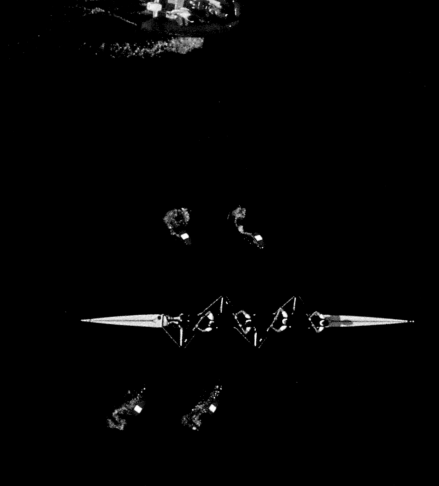

Contents

Arnolfo di Cambio's cathedral with its dome designed by Brunelleschi is the symbol of Florence.

Pages 6-7: *From the air, a single glance can embrace the heart of Florence, her history made tangible by her monuments: the octagonal Baptistery, the cathedral with its distinctive dome, and the Palazzo Vecchio. The Arno divides the city but her bridges unite it. One perceives the harmony of this city where, in the words of Leonardo Bruni, "nothing is disordered, nothing is without reason, nothing is without foundation."*

Pages 8-9: *The centre and its monuments, guardians of the past, are nowadays invaded by a rampant tourism which risks suffocating them.*

Pages 10-11: *The bridges of Florence: the Ponte Vecchio in the foreground and, beyond, the Ponte della Vittoria, the Ponte a Santa Trinità and the Ponte Amerigo Vespucci. From its very beginnings, the city has been engaged in a mighty struggle with the river that has invaded her many times. As old as the city herself, spanning her history and transformations, all the bridges, with the exception of the Ponte Vecchio, were destroyed during the last world war.*

IN THE SHADOW OF THE DOME

Florence is dying! These were the headlines announced around the world on the morning of November 4th, 1966. The city was flooded, drowning in mud, up to a height of four metres. The mud invaded houses, shops, libraries, museums and churches. From above, Florence appeared to be engulfed by a sticky, fuel oil-covered sea, and her end seemed nigh. Throughout the city and the Arno basin commerce, craft and industrial activity were disrupted. By a curious coincidence, the flood echoed that of November 4th, 1333, when the Arno broke its banks, washing away bridges and devastating the city. But Florence did not die.

In 1333, the populace reacted vigorously, and the catastrophe prompted the craft guilds to restore with new lustre the city which was soon to become the cradle of the Italian Renaissance. In 1966, it was claimed unabashedly, that the world needed Florence. And the world rallied its forces. Thanks to international aid and the tenacity and pride of the Florentine people, the city was saved once again. Today, photographed during a splendid springtime, it is indeed the "dream city" depicted by Mark Twain in his autobiography.

These superb pictures provide a synthesis, giving access to panoramic views and unexpected details normally hidden from sight. They give the impression that Florence is easy to approach, an impression that is misleading: Florence slips away, proffering her touristic "charms" while hiding her soul and *raison d'être*. The roar of traffic, the crowds cramming the tourist itineraries, the horrible souvenirs hawked on every street corner — all this does little to encourage (let alone inspire). It is unworthy of your expectations — and of Florence's culture and history.

It is possible, however, to go beyond the industrialised, impersonal, hurried tourism and to fully understand and appreciate Florence; it is even possible, sometimes, to have an emotional response so powerful as to provoke physical weakness. This indisposition has been observed by an Italian medical team studying numerous tourists and has been dubbed the "Stendhal syndrome". While visiting the church of Santa Croce, the celebrated French novelist was perturbed by the sight of the seventeenth century Volterrano frescoes in the Niccolini chapel: "...Volterrano's Sibyls gave me what was perhaps the most intense pleasure painting has ever given me. I was already in a sort of ecstasy due merely to being in Florence and being close to the great men whose tombs I had come to see. I was absorbed in the contemplation of this, seeing it from close up, for all intents and purposes touching it. I had reached that state of emotion where the lofty feelings inspired by great art meld with passionate feelings. Leaving Santa Croce, I had palpitations which, in Berlin, they call 'nerves'; I was drained and walked with the fear of falling." Many decades later, Henry James was to exclaim : "Lovely, very lovely, but it depresses me."

Before we throw ourselves into a whirlwind tour of museums, palaces, churches, cloisters, restaurants and shops, let us first — calmly — admire the view from atop a hill, from a bell-tower or from the air.

To grasp the urban fabric, one must understand the fundamental role played by the Arno, and the close relationship between city and countryside. One must have an overview of the original contours of Florence, with the river ploughing through its centre, protected to the north and south by hills. From the heights of Fiesole or from the garden of Sir Harold Acton's Villa La Pietra — situated on the former Via Bolognese, halfway to the Appenines — the city of Florence appears in the distance veiled by a bluish haze or bathed in sunlight. Beyond, the eye wanders to the low hill of San Miniato, to the terrace of the Piazzale Michelangelo — a vast nineteenth-century square — and, to the east, towards the Arno, the steep wooded hills of the Incontro and Villamagna. Whether there is haze or sunlight, always the cathedral dome, Brunelleschi's masterpiece, dominates the view, "raised against the sky, vast enough to cover all the Tuscan peoples with its shadow." So wrote Leon Battista Alberti, to whom we owe the façade of Santa Maria Novella. Vasari added: "The surrounding hills resemble it." We recognise Florence by her hills.

The Ponte Vecchio is built on the site of a Roman wooden bridge, replaced by a stone bridge that was destroyed by the Arno in 1177. In the thirteenth century, the bridge was rebuilt with the shops which make its silhouette immediately recognisable. The bridge is the monopoly of the goldsmiths: suspended above the water, this jewellery market is the most visited and most famous in the world.

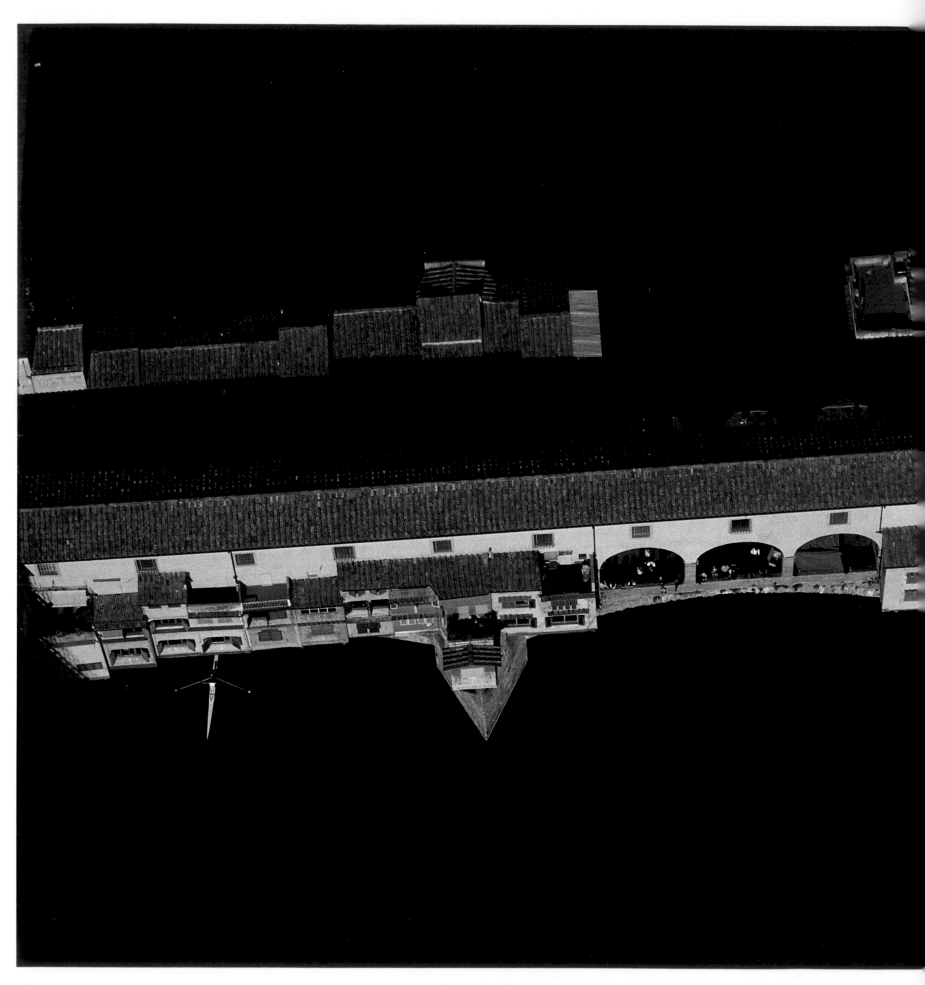

Passing from north to south, without lingering over the picture-postcard view of the Piazzale Michelangelo, the visitor arrives at the Belvedere fortress. The approach is magnificent, coming down from the hills by the Via San Leonardo: even if often travelled, this hill road remains one of the most magnificent in the world. Alternatively, climb up via the Costa San Giorgio, within a stone's throw of Michelangelo's fortifications. Once inside, walk around the ramparts of the star-shaped terrace. Built at the end of the sixteenth century by Buontalenti, the fort was the crowning feature of a defence system which served as a reminder to the Florentines, even though by this time they had already forsworn their republican liberties. It also represented the perfect link between the major urban elements: the Boboli Gardens and Pitti Palace to the left and, beyond, the Ponte Vecchio, the Palazzo della Signoria (or Palazzo Vecchio), the Duomo, the Santissima Annunziata and San Marco churches and, finally, another fortress known as "da Basso".

From the terrace of the Belvedere fortress, you overlook Florence and its tiled roofs and towers, the Palazzo Vecchio with its reddish tints, the greyish Uffizi... From here, reach out and virtually touch with your fingertips the city created by Arnolfo di Cambio, Filippo Brunelleschi and Michelangelo Buonarroti.

Before plunging into the depths of the city, become acquainted with her silhouette, her features, her colours... Here, one after another, are her bridges, her churches, her peaceful parks designed in the last century... There is the central area, mutilated, artificially reconstructed or, according to the inscription carved in the Piazza della Repubblica by the builders of last century, "given a new life"... And finally, there is the post-war architectural desert of the outskirts, destroying the delicate harmony between the city and countryside, that secret, intimate harmony that was the embodiment of the exquisite and inimitable charm of Florence.

Now, look up to the hills of the north to the Etruscan town of Fiesole. The Etruscans erected their fortifications in the hollow of a crescent-

The shops on the Ponte Vecchio were not always the preserve of the gold- and silversmiths. In 1442, the city rented them to the Arte dei Beccai (butchers' guild) and they became a meat market. The tiny houses protruding over the water, held up by lopsided supports, were added around 1495 and completely altered the appearance of the bridge. Subsequently, Vasari completely transformed it by incorporating it into the corridor linking the Palazzo Vecchio with the Pitti Palace: he covered the bridge and opened the three central portals. In 1593, the Signoria evicted the Beccai for having dirtied and degraded the bridge with their commerce. Gold and silver did not present this inconvenience. In 1856-57, Giuseppe Martelli, an enthusiastic supporter of the new architecture of the Crystal Palace in London, proposed that the bridge should be covered with a glass and metal roof under which people could stroll, have tea and listen to music. Happily, his idea never progressed beyond the planning stage.

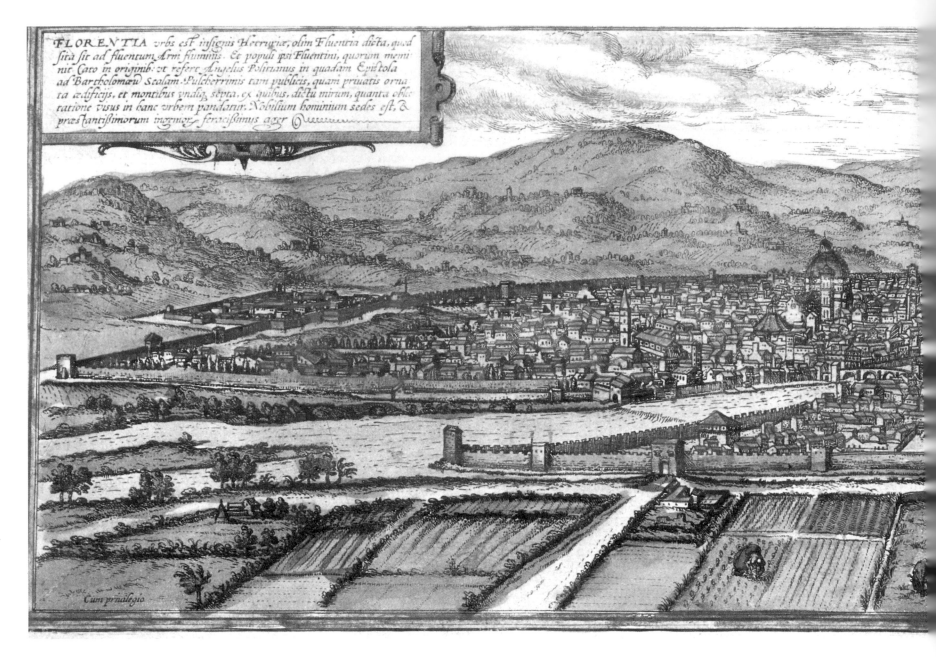

FLORENTIA orbis est insignis Hetruriae, olim Fluentia dicta, quod sita sit ad fluentum Arni fluminis. Et populi ipsi Fluentini, quorum meminit Cato in originib: vt refert Angelus Politianus in quadam Epistola ad Bartholomæū Scalam. Pulcherrimis tam publicis, quam priuatis ornata ædificijs, et montibus vndiq, septa, ex quibus, dictu mirum, quanta oblectatione visus in hanc vrbem pandatur. Nobilium hominium sedes est, & præstantissimorum ingenior: feracissimus ager

Cum priuilegio

A famous "veduta" (view) of Florence which appeared in the first volume of Civitates orbis terrarum, *published in Cologne in 1572.*

shaped pass, sheltered by hills descending gently towards Settignango and, on the other side, towards the Careggi and Sesto plains. Two thousand years ago, warriors, farmers and artisans left these hills to intermingle with Caesar's soldiers, giving birth to a race often in conflict with itself, a people renowned for its proud, obstinate and difficult nature.

The Etruscan civilisation left its mark upon these hills which are now behind us as we make our way along the Roman consular routes, flanked by cypresses, olive trees and vineyards, to the heart of the Chianti region, towards Siena and the ports of the Maremme. This landscape has remained unchanged, thanks to the knowledge of the Tuscan peasants and to the influence of the grand dukes of the eighteenth century. We begin to understand the degree to which the very heart of Florence and

the countryside around it are one and the same. The light, the colour of the stone, the work, the creative inspiration — all reflect one another. On the one hand is Nature "corrected" by artifice; on the other is an urban structure whose balance and measure recall the landscape of the surrounding hills.

The city seems to be an extension of the garden that became a symbol, first for Classical culture, then for the Renaissance: a meeting place for history and the universe. Montaigne, Goethe, Stendhal, Ugo Foscolo, Vittorio Alfieri, Giacomo Leopardi, Byron, Shelley, Chateaubriand, Emerson, Ruskin, Elisabeth and Robert Browning, D'Annunzio, Henry James and so many other artists have left us unforgettable portrayals, verbal or pictorial, of Florence. Each one of them saw a different aspect, but in every case, the Florence

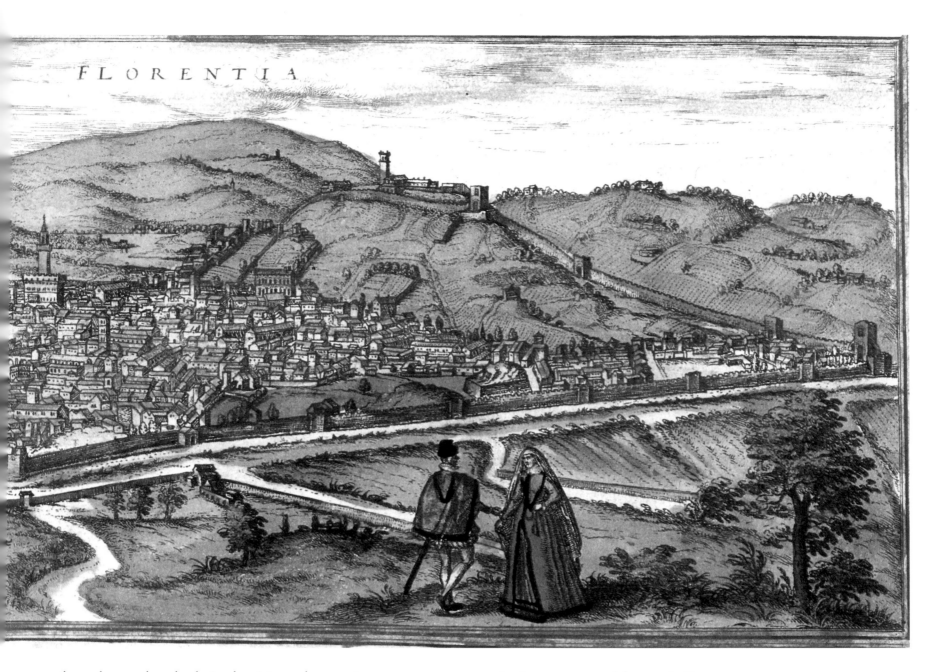

FLORENTIA

they observed and admired exists no longer. In their days the pace of life was slower, enabling them to penetrate, little by little, to the heart of things, to ensconce them firmly in their memory and imagination: this is lost forever. Today, a visitor stops in the Piazza della Signoria, opens his guidebook in the shade of the Loggia dell'Orcagna, walks around the Baptistery, awaits his turn to enter the Uffizi or strolls in the Boboli Gardens and his impressions are totally different. Florence is not simply a contrived tourist spot, although today, to go beyond the atmosphere of the anaemic city that the tourist industry strives to promote, a greater objectivity is required.

A photograph taken from the air has an enormous advantage. It can not only capture an aspect or an unusual detail, but can also produce a clear, uninterrupted image of a building or a monument. A picture snapped from a helicopter can burst with energy that is impossible to achieve in a photograph where angles have been minutely calculated. On the ground, one will then be able to fill out this image, being careful not to fall prey to the haste, the bustle and the noise.

Once the traces of the past have become sufficiently familiar, it is time to discover the other "souls" of Florence in order to grasp the spirit of the city, her character and, perhaps, her destiny. Let us get away from the cars which, as Franco Camarlinghi, in charge of cultural affairs in Florence, remarked, "have made the old routes unrecognisable". Let us avoid the "mass tourism which, nearly all year round, makes it impossible to get around in the black triangle of the obligatory itinerary — the Medici tombs, the Accademia and the Uffizi — a triangle transformed into a vast,

The caption in the top left corner mentions a letter from the poet Agnolo Poliziano to Bartolomeo Scala, stating that Florence was studded with splendid buildings, public as well as private, and that therein resided noble men of lofty spirit.

19

gaudy strip of restaurants and supermarkets of Italian footwear, for which (judging from the desperate struggle of bootmakers to get hold of old stores) there is an unending demand." This is the Florence which we regret, this is the soulless commercialism that we would like to see boycotted by the tourists themselves.

Far from the tourist routes, let us slowly wander through the dark, narrow streets of the centre or, even better, the Santa Croce district, so badly afflicted by the flood and now deserted by most of its inhabitants, and with them, their crafts, customs and lifestyle. Workshops have given way to "rustic" restaurants. The intellectual and mercantile bourgeoisie, the latter of more recent origin, now occupies the renovated upper storeys. But this neighbourhood, portrayed so movingly by Vasco Pratolini, has not been entirely destroyed. Even though the Piazza Santa Croce and thereabouts has been invaded by leather shops, there are still old shops to be found, such as Vivoli's, where the best ice cream in Italy is made and sold. Other small traders are also there with their used books and secondhand objects, and there are wine shops to savour, even now, a glass of Chianti accompanied by a good sausage. The voices under the Arco di San Pierino echo with the same timbre, the same inflections, the same ripostes, the same "Florentine" as fifty or a hundred years ago.

Beyond the Arno, beyond the Serucciolo (steep footpath) dei Pitti and the magnificent Via Maggio, is the Santo Spirito district with its shady piazza and, near the church, its gardens inspired by Brunelleschi. Here, the lives of ordinary people belong to the history of Florence, as do the smells of fine Tuscan specialities — grilled steak or ewes' milk cheese, *ribollita* (a vegetable soup eaten with cabbage and slices of bread) or chestnut cake. Behind the dark windows of some of the shops the old master bookbinders are hidden away. Only a couple of steps away from each other, the carpenter works next to the greengrocer, the potter next to the butcher, the antique dealer next to the little local restaurant which has always been there, perhaps even during the time of the grand dukes of Lorraine.

The flood could have given birth to a new conception of the city and its role. According to Franco Camarlinghi, "the disaster of the flood might have permitted the total rethinking of a city like Florence — both the old and the new — in terms of improved sanitation, renovation projects and the resolution of major problems." But instead, the centre found itself transformed into a shopping mall for tourists where there was no longer a place for the middle class, for the very people who had built the Florentine civilisation on a foundation of their small businesses and crafts. These people have been replaced by newcomers who see in the city's art and monuments nothing more than good opportunities for advertising and who, unlike their predecessors, are little concerned about investment in the future.

It is not a question of going back fifty years in time, when one could immediately distinguish the working classes and the middle classes from the "signori" (the nobles). Nor is it a question of minimising the cultural and economic role of the luxury industry: the ceramics and china, which became fashionable after the war and conquered Italy, beginning with Florence, giving worldwide fame to a great tradition; the antiques, among the finest in Italy, exhibited by dealers in beautiful shops in the Via Maggio, Via dei Fossi and the Borgo Ognissanti; the men's clothing, refined and tailored to British taste; the embroidery; the lingerie; the elegant metalwork. What is absolutely intolerable is to see the most beautiful streets of Florence, such as the Via Tornabuoni, reduced to mere display windows promoting the same labels and brands as the shops in London or New York.

The debate about the future of Florence continues. How can we save the city from the pollution which is asphyxiating it? Decentralisation, westerly development in the plain towards Prato, which now has gained the status and prestige of an important industrial centre; the creation of a technical and scientific university about seven miles from the centre; the development of tertiary activities and with them, the latest technology... These are possible solutions but they must not, however, make of Florence and its monuments

Pictures of Florence "include elements of an interest that goes beyond the local setting and becomes part of the history of urban and European iconography," wrote Giovanni Fanelli, architectural historian. Those who want to know more should visit the small Firenze com' erà (Florence of yesteryear) museum near the Duomo. There, one may savour the history of Florence in pictures: from large maps to vistas, engravings by Zocchi, paintings by Utens, pictures of the Ghetto and the Mercato Vecchio (Old Market), and Ottone Rosai's extraordinary portraits of his friends, major figures in the Italian cultural movement in the period between the two World Wars.

Above : This eighteenth century etching shows the Ponte a Santa Trinità. It was done by Zocchi to whom we owe a vast number of drawings, canvases and engravings depicting Florence and Tuscany at the time of the Grand Duke Piero Leopoldo.

Below : The great Corpus Christi procession in Florence. This anonymous etching is an inverted copy of an engraving by Zocchi.

simply an open air museum, crystallised in the past and cut off from new areas of activity.

There is, therefore, a problem of identity. I will never forget a recent exhibition of photographs by the Alinari Studio at the Belvedere. For most people the flood was already a distant memory, but everyone had its disastrous consequences in the back of their mind. The exhibition was seen by more than one hundred thousand visitors, mostly Florentines. They paused at length in front of the photographs, exchanging impressions and, sometimes, recollections. They discovered another Florence, poorer but more dignified, more humane. Here was a city not yet invaded by the roaring flow of traffic; on Sundays, people strolled at the Cascine, and the ladies had their portraits taken at the Alinari Studio in the Via Nazionale. These Florentines, among whom were many young people, were searching for the identity they had lost.

A few encouraging signs of change are to be seen. The centre has been closed to cars. Individuals and organisations of different viewpoints — intellectual, political and even economic — are trying to rethink Florence. Perhaps they will find the courage to affirm that the city's vocation is that of a great centre of cultural institutions and thus insist on the importance and autonomy of her two principal cultural institutions: the Central National Library and the Uffizi.

It is time to give a new life and a new coherence to the city, always keeping in mind the success of artistic events such as exhibitions featuring Henry Moore, the Macchiaioli (an important movement in Italian painting, 1850-1880), the Medicis or the Etruscan civilisation, and without forgetting the development of institutes set up by foreign universities. The Florentines have always insisted upon affirming their cultural identity but, unfortunately, they have never been entirely successful. If, however, the city is to be, at long last, competently run, decisions and policies should by guided by deeper reflection on the future role of culture in Florence.

The Baptistery, the Campanile and the Duomo seen from the church of the S.S. Annunziata. The sweep of the dome crowns the religious centre of the communal and mediaeval city. "Florentines liked the Baptistery because, for them, it was a symbol of historic pride; the Baptistry was also a temple dedicated to Saint John, the patron saint of their city. Finally, it was the paragon of the style to which their taste aspired..." (Luciano Berti, Tutta la città e la sua arte, *1979)*

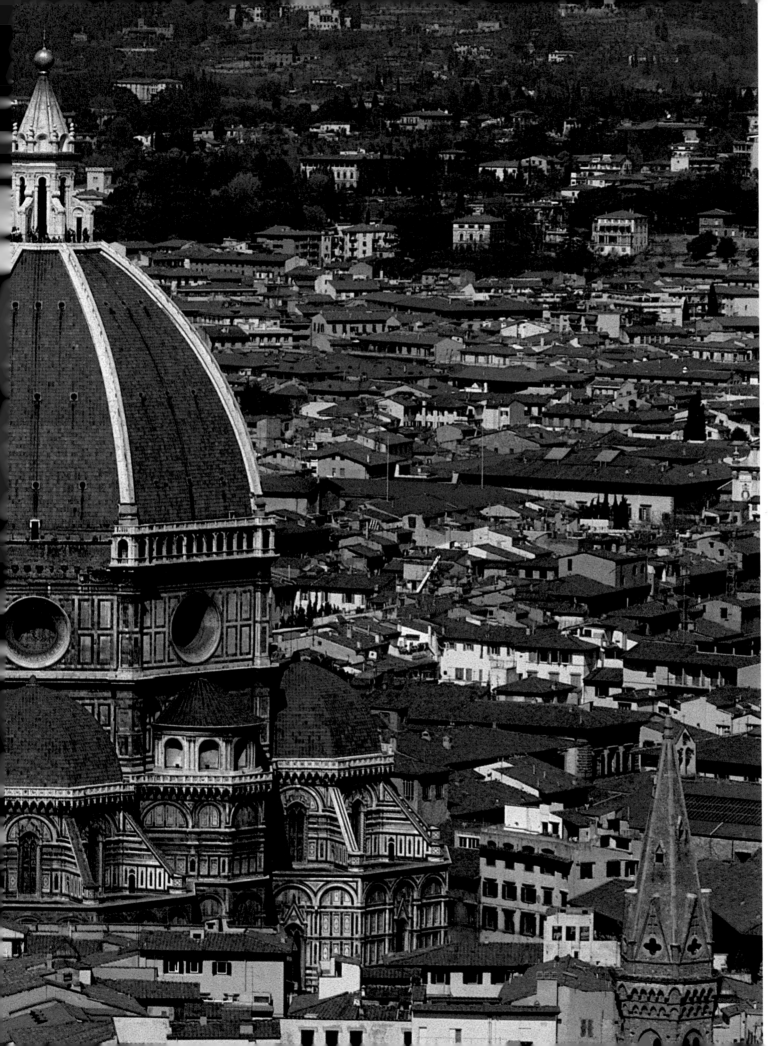

The Duomo rises above the site of the former cathedral of Santa Reparata. The immense architectural undertaking was entrusted to Arnolfo di Cambio with one stipulation: that the Duomo must be "the highest and of the most sumptuous magnificence", and must worthily represent the city which had become so prosperous and powerful. In 1471, when the golden globe topped by a cross was finally raised to the summit of the dome, one hundred and seventy-five years had elapsed since the beginning of its construction. The cost of the Duomo had attained the exorbitant sum of eighteen million gold florins or approximately two hundred million pounds sterling.

THE CRADLE OF THE RENAISSANCE

Little is known about the period between the actual founding of Florentia as a Roman colony, in 59 B.C., and the year 1000. But it is certain that, as of around the mid-thirteenth century, Florence came strikingly to life: the centre of the city, constructed over a period of three hundred years, abounds with masterpieces dating from this time. It is as if the city knew that she was destined to dominate the European stage for the next three centuries.

Throughout a thousand years of war, famine, destruction, barbarian invasions, Byzantine, Lombard and Carolingian domination the proud spirit of Florence remained indomitable.

In the middle of the thirteenth century, feudal structures were on the verge of collapse. In the city, towers sometimes reaching a height of seventy metres were still being erected, but their fate was linked to that of the two rival factions: the Guelphs, who supported the papal power, and the Ghibellins, partisans of imperial power. Following defeats, the height of the towers diminished, some of them even being completely destroyed.

A new conception of life, of public administration, of business and the arts was in the process of imposing itself. Castles in the environs were being abandoned, often to be replaced by villas belonging to rich merchants. In the place of unwelcoming urban residences, more comfortable palaces were being constructed, inhabited by those whose power stemmed not from the destructive force of arms but from money and a spirit of enterprise. This was a city different from the old Florence: an austere and parsimonious city, regretted by Cacciaguida, forebear of Dante:

Fiorenza dentro de la cerchia antica,
(...) si stava in pace, sobria e pudica.
(*Paradis*, XV, 96-99)
(Florence, in her ancient walls,
Lived peacefully, sober and modest.)

On a number of occasions, the city ramparts were torn down in order to be moved further out. The last time, building began in 1284 and finished in 1333, the year of the terrible flood, enclosing a territory far greater than in the past, large enough, indeed, to hold the population of Florence up until the second half of the nineteenth century.

The sites of religious and civil buildings were also fitted into a long-term plan, displaying a will and a confidence in the future which were to characterise Florentine culture until the end of the sixteenth century. The imposing mass of the cathedral, crowned by its dome, was the first indication of the unbridled pride of the Florentine people: Santa Maria del Fiore (or simply "Duomo", before being dedicated to the saint) dominates the city even though spiritual and civil meeting places such as Santa Croce, Santa Maria Novella and the Palazzo Vecchio, symbolise as fully the city's vitality.

In the Middle Ages, the Florentine style never took on the grave — and sometimes, even dramatic — aspect of the Gothic style. Here, Classically-inspired balance and lightness prevail. Cimabue himself started from the classic principles of Byzantine art, but gave an unprecedented relief to the crucified Christ in Santa Croce. Then, Giotto boldly developed the innovations of his master. Within this cultural atmosphere, a perfect continuity extended from the Middle Ages through Humanism, finally reaching an apotheosis with the Renaissance.

Obviously, at some points along the way, there were moments more intense than others. In these cases, a work demonstrated a firmness, a force or certainty borne of logic such that its very evidence would not be questioned for centuries. Only when Man begins to mould history, does Heaven approach the Earth. One of the great examples of a Florentine "creator" in a republic bursting with vitality was Arnolfo di Cambio. Straddling the thirteenth and fourteenth centuries, he became the organiser, the planner of a society in full mutation which was bringing about its own rebirth and renewal through the arts.

Florence was already rich in Romanesque churches such as the Santi Apostoli, founded around the year 1000, Santo Stefano, the Badia and San Miniato al Monte. The new religious orders — preaching and mendicant — profoundly influenced the community by opening the first schools and beginning the construction of monumental ensembles such as the church of Santa Maria Novella. Arnolfo di Cambio was entrusted with the project of Santa Croce, whose bare interior of graceful curves no longer resembles the somber Gothic style to which, however, it belongs. But the most remarkable structure is — in the words of Dante — the "beautiful San Giovanni", the octagonal Baptistery facing the cathedral of Santa Reparata. Probably founded in the fifth century, the Baptistery is the spiritual centre of the Florentine community. The interior is in the Byzantine style, whereas the exterior is faced in the typical green and white marble which Arnolfo would later use for Santa Maria del Fiore.

And Florence continued to grow. Despite insurrections, destruction, military defeats and changes of government, the city enjoyed an enormous economic clout. The letter of credit, invented by Florentine bankers, was used with increasing frequency, and her currency, the gold florin, was accepted throughout Europe. At the end of the thirteenth century, the "arts" (or guilds) affirmed their power, underlining the decadence of the nobility: merchants and craftsmen (wool, silk, silver), artists and professional people would be responsible for Florence's splendour for the next two centuries. During this period, urban renewal and construction projects were innumerable. In 1300, the population topped one hundred thousand — half that of Paris and double that of London. Florence would not exceed this figure until the nineteenth century.

Arnolfo di Cambio was now working on Santa Croce and restructuring the Badia Fiorentina. He began to enlarge Santa Reparata (the first cathedral) and linked the religious ensemble of the Duomo and the Baptistery to the Piazza della Signoria by designing the first part of the Palazzo della Signoria. The massive lower part of this splendid, imposing sandstone palace was capable of withstanding attacks, while the upper floors, pierced by tall windows, gave an impression of greater lightness.

With disputes, hesitation and instability, democratic regimes (officially tied to the Empire or to the papacy) alternated with tyrannies. As had the Medicis before them, the representatives of the Florentine people governed from what would later become known as the Palazzo Vecchio. This palace was the symbol of civil might.

After the death of Arnolfo, work on the Duomo continued, but at a slower pace, until Giotto took charge in 1334. The master saw the bell-tower as an opportunity to end his dazzling career on a triumphant note (in fact, he died three years later). His solution, with its geometric patterns of different colours of marbles, niches, statues and openwork, was thoroughly original. The bas-reliefs, most of which were executed by Andrea Pisano under the supervision of the church fathers, attest to the industrial and commercial activity as well as to the role of the artisans who ensured the city's prosperity. John Ruskin believed this to be one of Europe's finest examples of man guided by heavenly inspiration.

By this time, the Middle Ages had been relegated well and truly to the past. Heaven no longer crushed Man. The fifteenth century began with a competition in which two artists, both barely twenty years old, confronted each other for the commission at stake: the doors of the Baptistery. This fascinating artistic duel between Lorenzo Ghiberti and Filippo Brunelleschi was keenly followed by all of Florence. The latter presented a powerfully theatrical and innovative project, while the former was more conciliatory, adapting his design to the still-prevalent Gothic taste of the times — and that of the jury. He won the competition and, in some twenty years, finished the doors while, at the same time, creating the most important centre of sculpture of the Renaissance.

He was also to complete another door facing the eastern façade of the Duomo. But there, he conjured up an illusion of vast space based on perspective without, however, abandoning the harmonious balance which marked his earlier triumph. Michelangelo would later contend that these doors were "worthy of standing at the entrance to Paradise". Henceforth, they would be known as the Gates of Paradise.

Meanwhile Brunelleschi cleverly managed to win for himself the boldest, most extraordinary project of all: the dome of the Duomo. An architectural and engineering marvel, an ingenious link in the spacial relationship between the city and the hills, a superb work of art and definitive symbol of Florence...here was the first lucid and exalted symbol of the new man: the Renaissance Man.

Face to face, the Florentine Romanesque Baptistery, so close to its Classical and Roman origins, and the elegant Gothic Campanile, described by the Emperor Charles V as "a precious jewel which should be preserved under a bell-glass."

"I never pass in front of Giotto's Campanile without my heart becoming lighter, as if a celestial beam had descended upon me," wrote James Jackson Jarves, one of the first collectors of Italian primitives, in 1867. "When, sad and ailing, I go to the Duomo and walk about, I am comforted by its presence, not because the idea of religious life is associated with it, but because in it I see the greatness of the human spirit triumphant in its faith in the infinite..."

From the late Middle Ages to the communal period, Florence enjoyed an architectural continuity which is perfectly summed up by the "dialogue" between the two monuments dearest to the Florentine people and most representative of their identity: San Giovanni's Baptistery, an obligatory reference to earlier Romanesque structures, and Giotto's Campanile whose exquisite delicacy is shown in this illustration.

"Arnolfo's project foresaw the union of the longitudinal naves with the central core covered by the dome... It is also to Arnolfo that we owe the idea of relating the green and white decoration of the Baptistery to that of the Duomo... The whole was conceived according to the scale of the city within the perimeter of the new ramparts; these principles were to be pushed even further by Brunelleschi and the construction of the dome, far higher than Arnolfo had planned."
(*Lara Vinca Masini,* Itinerari per Firenze, *1981).*

Brunelleschi had total control over the entire construction project, even conceiving the mechanical elements needed to hoist the construction materials. The considerable technical problems he had to resolve in order to erect the dome have been the subject of numerous books. For the conception of his system of "umbrella spokes", Brunelleschi was apparently inspired by Roman construction techniques: the dome was able to support itself as it was erected, thanks to the counterforce of the ribs.

33

The Renaissance conferred on stone a grandeur in comparison with which man appeared very small indeed.

The camera lense is mesmerised by the play of space and pattern on the Duomo, the cool white marble contrasting with the warm tones of the tiles. Seen from below, the enormous bulk of the church seems to squeeze in with difficulty amongst the houses which surround it; seen from above, its architecture imposes itself with superb prominence and impressive power.

The Palazzo Vecchio was known by various names, according to the events of history: Palazzo dei Priori, then della Signoria and finally Ducale. This was the second civil structure, after the Palazzo del Podestà (currently known as the Bargello), that the city constructed at its apogee. By its size and volume, the Palazzo Vecchio would stand out amongst the noblemen's towers, the guild halls and the houses of the wealthy merchants. Arnolfo di Cambio drew up the plans, and the core was built between 1299 and 1314. The tower, rectangular like the Palazzo it dominates, is ninety-four metres high. It is topped by a gallery which juts out and, further up, by a bronze steeple crowned with the Marzocco, a lion rampant, one of the symbols of the city. Emphasising power as an integral part of the city's defence network, the tower also served as a prison.

Florentines were sceptical about the statue of Neptune carved by Ammannati during the second half of the sixteenth century. They dubbed it "Biancone" (the fat white one), finding it misproportioned for its setting, and made up the following epigram: "O Ammannato, Ammannato, what a beautiful piece of marble you've ruined." The bronze statues of satyrs and sea gods were also designed by Ammannati, but cast by Giambologna.

The glorious Piazza della Signoria, marred by the seemingly endless works. Although they are inconvenient for the tourists, they nonetheless are bringing to light vestiges of the city dating from the Roman era and the late Middle Ages.

"The Santa Croce district, one of the best preserved of Florence, with its mediaeval palaces, narrow alleys and splendid monuments dominated by the church of Santa Croce, temple of the Italic tribe..." (Onorio Gelli and Geno Pampaloni, Firenze, 1986). Designed by Arnolfo di Cambio for the Franciscans, the church, begun in 1294, was consecrated in 1443. On the 4th of November 1966, the Arno flooded the city, and the Santa Croce district was one of the worst hit. The muddy waters rose up to four metres in the fifteenth-century cloisters of the Basilica, while the devastating current swept away priceless books, manuscripts and incunabula from the nearby reserves of the National Library. Thousands of books were destroyed while others survived, thanks to the generous intervention of hundreds of young volunteers, both Italian and foreign. In the Santa Croce museum, the crucifix by Cimabue, master of Giotto, was knocked over, much of its paint dissolving in the mud of the Arno.

The façade, completed during the last century in neo-Gothic style, dominates the piazza which, for centuries, has been one of the Florentines' favourite meeting-places. They came to hear Franciscans preach or watch a match of Florentine calcio. This sport, similar to soccer, is passionately loved by the inhabitants who have never forgotten a match played in 1530, in which they decisively trounced a team made up of the soldiers of Charles V who had seized Florence. Nowadays, this ancient game has become a spectacle played in colourful Renaissance costume.

The very old basilica of San Lorenzo is, in its actual form, the result of pillage: in 1418, the
church prior obtained permission from the city to expropriate part of the district — the site of the
current transept — in order to enlarge the old church on the side of the apse. The prior did not
shrink from demolishing several houses, as well as a square and a street. The work, entrusted to
Filippo Brunelleschi, began in 1421. Interrupted by the death of the master, it was continued
under the direction of Michelozzo, architect to the Medicis. The entire church is an ode to the
glory of that family: the Old Sacristy by Brunelleschi, with tondos by Donatello, houses the tomb
of Piero and Giovanni de' Medicis by Verrocchio; the New Sacristy by Michelangelo, encloses the
tombs of the Medicis and the Princes' Chapel, in which semi-precious stones glitter. Next door is
another tribute to the Medicis: the Laurentian Library, Michelangelo's architectural masterpiece.

San Lorenzo is one of those great Florentine churches in which art and history are at one with the day-to-day life of a bustling neighbourhood. The market, of which we can see the double row of covered stands, is heavily visited, especially by tourists.

*The Arno today flows beneath a stream of automobiles which
have invaded the embankments and the entire city. At the time of
the guilds, the Arno supplied the woollen and leather industries with water.
The stinking, noxious air was the high price the inhabitants paid for the
prosperity of their city.*

On the water, and above. From the arches of the Ponte Vecchio, tourists gaze at oarsmen gliding swiftly by. The Società dei Canottieri (Rowing Club) of Florence has its headquarters close by, on the banks beneath the Uffizi.

Overlooking Vasari's passage, this is the view that entrances Lucy, heroine of Room with a View, *when she has just arrived in Florence. The film, adapted from E.M. Forster's novel, is recommended to all those who yearn for Florence.*

The Ponte Vecchio was spared by the Nazi mines, but at either end, the houses of Por Santa Maria, Borgo San Jacopo, the Via Guicciardini and the Via de' Bardi, were demolished or seriously damaged. They were later reconstructed in their original style. Here, as in most of the rest of the city, yellow-ochre plaster is prevalent, a colour which seems to glow in the light of dawn and dusk.

At dusk, according to the poets, the waters of the Arno turn to liquid silver. In the foreground, the Ponte alle Grazie, followed by the Ponte Vecchio, the Ponte a Santa Trinità, the Ponte alla Carraia, the Ponte da Verrazzano and the Ponte alla Vittoria.

THE GOLDEN AGE

Bathed in the soft light of spring, the mediaeval reddish sandstone of Arnolfo di Cambio's city does not overshadow the white and greyish tints of the monuments of Brunelleschi. The latter are particularly striking when seen from above, masterpieces in the middle of crowded squares, standing out from the tangle of streets: the façade of the Ospedale degli Innocenti (Foundlings' Hospital), the perfectly proportioned Piazza S. S. Annunziata, or San Lorenzo which houses the marvellous Sagrestia Vecchia (the Old Sacristy), Santo Spirito, set back a bit, and the Pazzi Chapel at Santa Croce.

In these works, the Renaissance spirit attains its perfection and modernity. Even though he took ancient history as his starting point, Brunelleschi thought, designed and invented abstract spaces with squares and circles, cubes or hemispheres. He rationalised the real world, recreating it geometrically. He subjected religiosity to human rules as would, each in his own fashion, the two other great protagonists of early fifteenth-century art, Masaccio and Donatello, both of whom were friends of his.

The dome, to which Brunelleschi devoted most of his life, thus summed up his work while becoming the very symbol of the centuries making up the Golden Age of Florence. The great art historian Giulio Carlo Argan wrote: "The dome no longer weighs on the structure, but hovers in the air, balanced and swollen, the portions of the roof stretched between the ribs like cloth between the ribs of an umbrella..., it is the pivot around which the districts and streets of the city are organised. It dominates and characterises the city landscape and evokes the hills..."

Donatello would be as great and as dynamic an innovator. From Classical beginnings, he arrived at a new, prophetic kind of sculpture in which the analysis of space evolved towards expressionism: figures were reduced to spectres, and humanistic harmony ceded to the drama of history. His wooden sculpture of Mary Magdalen in the Baptistery "is the hallucinating image of an anguish which, today we call existentialism", wrote Argan. Every bit as dramatic are the pulpits of San Lorenzo. It is as if

Donatello, awaking from the Humanist dream, re-entered history and saw nothing but its suffering and crimes. He announced another Florence, a city whose liberty would fall into the hands of the great families; a city where, the initial "enlightened" domination of the Medicis would give way to the tyranny of their descendants. A city which would experience the Apocalypse of Savonarola, and whose artists would go through a period of crisis: be it the exacerbated spiritualism of late Botticelli, Leonardo abandoning Florence for a richer and more "realistic" Milan, or the delusion of Michelangelo following the collapse of moral and political ideals which accompanied the return of the Medicis — supported by foreign armies. Urban culture turned in upon itself or gave in to the temptation of alchemy. The Studiolo of Francesco I is a perfect example of this, as are the automatons of the Boboli Gardens and the Medici villas with their intangible "reality", made up of the play of light and shade, of dreams and nightmares. These dreams and nightmares which occupied the family until the last of the line, the feeble-minded Gian Gastone, disappeared, opening the way to the new Austrian House of Lorraine.

Florence was the capital of the Renaissance. In the fifteenth and sixteenth centuries, her poets, philosophers, painters, sculptors and architects were famous throughout Europe. The city continued to evolve and to be enriched with new masterpieces, but henceforth, it was no longer the guilds but the great banking families who spurred on the development.

The fabulous, tormented destiny of the Medicis began with Giovanni di Bicci who, from his first residence in the Piazza del Duomo, was able to follow the progress of the dome. It was he who began to finance the reconstruction of San Lorenzo, entrusting the Sacristy project to Brunelleschi in 1421. Giovanni was to be interred there, the first of a long line of Medicis. His son Cosimo, known as the Elder, succeeded him, inheriting his passion for building. He asked Michelozzo to reconstruct the convent of San Marco whose library was the first to open its doors to a scholarly public. Cosimo the Elder also engaged Michelozzo to build the palace in the Via Larga where the Medicis would live until

The bell-tower of the Duomo, built between 1436 and 1471, "corresponds to a will which is constant with Brunelleschi: to deny the material consistency of an architectonic mass, in order to create a structure which generates space." (Giovanni Fanelli, Brunelleschi, 1977). The soaring dome remains the most beautiful testimony to the Florentine Renaissance.

The Fortezza da Basso (the Lower Fortress, formerly the San Giovanni Fortress) is a masterpiece of sixteenth-century military and civil architecture. Designed between 1534 and 1535 by Antonio da Sangallo the Younger, its imposing keep incorporates the Porta a Faenza (Faenza Gate) which dates from the thirteenth century. Abandoned for centuries, then used as a barracks, it was outfitted in 1965 to house the Mostra dell' Artigianato (Crafts Exhibition), fashion shows and other commercial events. The northern façade of the fortress is softened by a nineteenth-century garden, created, like the grand avenues, at a time when Florence was a capital.

moving into the Palazzo Vecchio.

Plots, illness, premature deaths, exiles and sieges marked the rise of the Signoria, which reached its apogee with Lorenzo the Magnificent. At the risk of squandering the family fortune, Lorenzo enriched the Medici art collections and spurred the culture to its greatest refinement by surrounding himself with such figures as Marsilio Ficino, Alberti, Poliziano and Pico della Mirandola. Himself a philosopher and poet, he protected and encouraged the great artists of the day: Verrocchio, Pollaiuolo, Botticelli, Signorelli, Perugino, Ghirlandaio, Giuliano da Sangallo and Michelangelo. The Medici Palace brimmed with works of art which were willingly shown to cultured visiting foreigners.

The Medici government disappeared with the invasion of Italy by Charles VIII; the first Republic, whose secretary would be Niccolo Machiavelli, was born. Florence then experienced an extraordinary period of freedom which was also beneficial to the arts. Leonardo and Michelangelo returned from exile, as did Raphael. Regardless of different points of view, certainties and concerns, all were inspired by nature, searching to identify faith with history.

There was a crisis in values — social, religious and cultural — linked with the consequences of Christopher Columbus's discovery of America; the New World explorations of Vespucci and Giovanni da Verrazzano; and the Protestant Reformation. At the same time as the foundation of the Academies (linguistic and botanical), of anatomical collections, and of centres of mathematical and astronomical studies, a new science was being developed, going so far even as to recant Galileo. In short, the seeds of the modern world were being sown, and even the artists were aiding the fledgling Republic: Michelangelo had begun the fortification of the walls above the Arno.

The Medicis returned to power in 1512, aided by one of their own, Pope Leo X. They were again banished, only to return definitively after the siege of Florence in 1530, thus crushing all hope of democracy.

In 1540, Cosimo I left the family palace to move into the Palazzo della Signoria, a way of affirming his absolute power over the city. The Medici family included popes, they were related to Charles V, and Catherine and Maria would become queens of France. The works linked with their name are legendary: the Medici tombs at San Lorenzo, with their sculptures by Michelangelo, notable for their expressiveness and extreme plasticity; the Laurentian Library, also by Michelangelo, boasting an architecture of unequalled perfection, housing the vast collection of books and manuscripts amassed by Cosimo the Elder and Lorenzo the Magnificent; the Uffizi and Vasari's corridor linking it with the Pitti Palace, an ingenious idea of Cosimo I's, who after having named his son Francesco I Prince Regent, had moved into the Pitti Palace. The corridor provided a direct passageway between the two palaces, thus avoiding having to go through the city. The Uffizi, literally "offices" (their function at the time, as well as being a workshop for the decorative arts and a theatre), were opened to the public as of the end of the sixteenth century.

The last bigoted or depraved Medici grand dukes died out, leaving the government to the House of Lorraine, it being understood that the fabulous Medici treasures would remain the property of Florence. The Lorraine dynasty was to govern Tuscany for a century (not counting the Napoleonic interlude), up until the declaration of Italian independence in 1859. Meanwhile, in the midst of a great social and economic upheaval, a great reformer was distinguishing himself in Florence and all of Tuscany: Pietro Leopoldo.

For centuries, Florence had been a great "factory", where people worked with wool, silk and leather, wove and dyed, where the house was one with the shop, and rich neighbourhoods intermingled with the poor; now it lost its vastness as people moved out to the country. Few artisans' workshops remained, while the court, now located at the Pitti Palace, and the factories, installed in the Uffizi at the time of Ferdinando I, began to concentrate on more refined crafts, such as mosaics, sculpted picture frames, cabinet-making, gilding, weaving the cloth for liturgical garments, gold- and silverwork. These activities still flourish today, as in the eighteenth century, thanks to the admiration of foreigners...and their purchases.

The Piazza della
S.S.Annunziata, one of the
most beautiful of
Renaissance Florence. It is
bordered by the church
built by the Serviti and
reconstructed by Michelozzo
in the sixteenth century, the
Palazzo della Confraternita
dei Serviti, and the Spedale
degli Innocenti (foundlings'
hospital, 1419-1426) with its
famous gallery. Brunelleschi
incorporated the hospital
into the existing decor of the
piazza, using a judicious
blend of pure geometric
forms. One of the most
beloved buildings in
Florence, it was, in fact, the
first hospital in Italy devoted
to taking in abandoned
children, the "nocentini" as
they were called. The blue-
and-white medallions, one
of Italian art's most
marvellous odes to
childhood, were added by
Andrea della Robbia
in 1487.

The Palazzo della Confraternita des Serviti, by Antonio da Sangallo the Elder and Baccio d'Agnolo (1518). Like a mirror, it pays hommage to Brunelleschi's foundlings' hospital on the opposite side of the piazza.

The Santo Spirito (Holy Ghost) church is well worth crossing the Arno for. It is located in a part of the city which, more than any other, has kept its mediaeval and Renaissance atmosphere. With its narrow, winding streets and little piazzas, it is both animated and picturesque. The Piazza Santo Spirito is dominated by the unadorned façade of Brunelleschi's church. Construction began around 1450 and continued after the death of the architect, his plans being faithfully respected.

*San Frediano al Cestello
is a former Cistercian abbey
church, "cestello" being the
Florentine deformation of
"Cîteaux", the seat of the
order. Reconstructed in the
seventeenth century by A.M.
Ferri, it represents a happy
marriage of Classicism and
Florentine Baroque. Vasco
Pratolini set his novel*
Le ragazze di San Frediano
*in the shadow of this
church, in the district of the
same name. An authentic
Florentine author of the last
century, Pratolini describes
the common people with
lyricism and affection, while
lucidly analysing the social
problems with which the city
inhabitants had to cope.*

Santa Maria del Carmine. The building itself is unexceptional and furthermore was damaged by fire in 1771. But it is a veritable pilgrimage site for lovers of painting: it is here, in the Brancacci Chapel, that Masaccio, between 1425 and 1427, developed Renaissance painting and affirmed a new way of thinking, seeing... and living. His work, at long last restored, now shines in all its splendour.

The imposing gallery of the Ospedale di Santa Maria Nuova, on the piazza of the same name, is one of the best examples of Florentine urban planning in the sixteenth and seventeenth centuries. Attributed to Buontalenti, its elegant yet vigorous design is of a typically Florentine sobriety.

Even if the name and the statue of the Piazza Mentana date from the Risorgimento (1815-1870), the area belongs to the Middle Ages, with its maze of narrow streets, its tower-houses and artisans' shops. Leaving the Arno at the Ponte alle Grazie, one enters a city that belongs to another age.

We are at the beginning of the Via del Prato, near the Borgo Ognissanti. According to a nineteenth-century guide book, this curious structure, which the Florentines baptised "the Rotonda", was used in the past for "exhibitions of large panoramas" such as the one depicting Naples. Before that, it was supposedly a training ground for wrestling and physical exercise. The rivalry of different factions often turned into real combat, leaving many dead or wounded.

Santa Maria Novella and its piazza represent one of Florence's
highpoints, where art and history prevail over the turbulence
of today's lifestyle. "For this Gothic church, Alberti, in a stroke
of genius, rediscovered the geometric marquetry of Florentine
Romanesque... but he worked the Romanesque theme according to the
principles of Vitruvius and modular composition..." (Giulio Carlo
Argan, Storia dell'arte italiana, vol. II). Magnificent volutes
relate the façade to the tympanum in which is set a huge sun,
referring to the passage of Hermes. Ficino himself pronounced that
"the Sun is the greatest of the celestial gods and father of all things".
One wonders if the Dominicans of Santa Maria Novella understood—
and approved of— this strange syncretism of pagan and Christian beliefs.

The portico of the Uffizi and the beginning of Giorgio Vasari's "Corridoio". This extraordinary passageway which crosses the Arno by the Ponte Vecchio, was built for Cosimo I. With the Uffizi, all major civil and political activities were regrouped around the Palazzo Ducale (later the Palazzo Vecchio) and its piazza. The Corridoio linked the seat of political power with the Pitti Palace, the ducal and royal residence, thus definitively affirming the Medici hegemony over Florence.

A skiff follows the Lungarno Vespucci, an embankment running along the edge of one of Florence's most elegant residential neighbourhoods.

The Pitti Palace, "huge...like some ghost of a ruder Babylon... Generations of Medicis have stood at these closed windows, embroidered and brocaded according to their period, and held fêtes champêtres and floral games on the greensward, beneath the mouldering hemicycle..." (Henry James, Italian Hours, 1909).
Today, as at the time of James, the Pitti Palace houses great masterpieces in the Palatine Gallery and the Gallery of Modern Art (although here, "modern" art dates from a few decades ago). Silverware, porcelain, carriages and excellent temporary exhibitions make a visit well worthwhile.

Luca Pitti's residence, designed by Brunelleschi in 1440 and completed by his student Cosimo Fancelli, represents a new conception of the nobleman's palace, no longer an integral part of the city and the street, but superbly isolated and surrounded by a scenic space, nature taking the place of the piazza. Eleonore of Toledo, wife of Cosimo I who acquired it in 1549, knew the spot "could become a splendid palace, exemplary of the lavishness Spanish taste seemed to require... Cosimo encouraged the project, conscious of the symbolic value of this vital place... His sons would extend the axis across the entire city, anchoring it to the two cardinal points represented by the Belvedere and Lower Fortresses."(Ludovico Zorzi, in Il luogo teatrale *a Firenze, 1975)*

"The Boboli Gardens are not large — you wonder how compact little Florence finds room for them within her walls...You may cultivate in them the fancy of their solemn and haunted character, of something faint and dim and even, if you like, tragic, in their prescribed, their functional smile...the place contains, thank goodness — or at least thank the grave, the infinitely-distinguished traditional taste of Florence — no cheerful trivial object, neither parterres, nor pagodas, nor peacocks, nor swans..." (Henry James, Italian Hours, 1909).

Between the Porta Romana and the Piazzale Torquato Tasso, ramparts conceal the romantic gardens of the Villa Torrigiani. Here English style is dominant, without completely effacing the stamp of neo-Classicism. This enclosed garden represents the "the typical hortus conclusus *in the midst of which a romantic green space... evokes sensations located beyond time and space..."*
(Francesco Bandini, Su e giù per le antiche mura, *Florence, 1983)*

The turret of the Torrigiani Gardens, designed by G. Baccani between 1820 and 1830, was one of the first examples of the eclecticism prevalent in the last century. Baccani also designed the neo-Gothic bell-tower of Santa Croce.

THE HAZARDS OF URBANISM

Florence possesses a marvellous museum — often overlooked by tourists — featuring Florence of yesteryear (Firenze com'era), in the days before it was deformed by city-planning projects. Most of its exhibits date from before the year 1865, when the city became the capital of the new kingdom of Italy, from the years before the expansion of the lower middle class at the turn of the century and the burgeoning of the suburbs after World War II.

Etchings by Zocchi from the eighteenth century, surprising views by the Flemish artist Utens, drawings of the Mercato Vecchio (Old Market) and the Ghetto — these recreate for the visitor harmonious scenes from a far-distant past.

A few changes took place from the eighteenth century onwards, and during the fifteen years of Napoleon's occupation, under the rule of Elisa Bacciochi, his sister. But for more than a century, no major programme was undertaken due to reduced economic resources. Metallic architecture made a timid appearance. As always, the accent was on quality, even for low-income housing for weavers of the Barbano district.

Five years after the stealthy departure of Leopoldo of Lorraine, the capital of the new kingdom was transferred to Florence. And, naturally, there had to be room for a king, his court, the government, in short, for some fifty thousand people in a city whose population, at the time, numbered but twice that. Roads were enlarged or lengthened, while what were supposed to be aesthetic improvements took place. In 1863, the façade of Santa Croce was renovated (as was, alas, that of the Duomo, later on). Thus disappeared "one of the great silent walls which dominate the principal piazzas of Florence and which, fundamentally, correspond more closely to the Florentine mentality than any ornamentation" (Giovanni Fanelli, *Firenze*, 1980). A few of these unadorned façades have thankfully escaped the catastrophic "improvements" of the eclectic artists of the nineteenth century: these real marvels are hidden around the Piazzas Santo Spirito, San Lorenzo and San Frediano in Cestello.

After the announcement of the capital's transfer, rents soared. In the ensuing panic, the municipal administration ordered the construction of new housing, eventually to include even prefabricated units. Plans were drawn up for a larger city. In the space of two months, the architect Poggi finalised a project for an overall restructuring of the city, which would engulf the communes on the outskirts.

Inspired by the examples of Paris and Vienna, the outer city walls were demolished, followed by the creation of a ring-road and the opening up of large spaces and the ramp of the Piazzale Michelangelo. While generally these undertakings were worthy, they are not exempt from criticism. What remains absolutely unjustifiable is the total destruction, in the historic city centre, of the Mercato Vecchio and the Jewish Ghetto, the very site of the foundations of Roman Florence. Neither towers nor churches, guildhalls nor remains of the Roman city were spared. Reconstruction projects were discussed at length but not many were realised. However, the legacy of the first half of the century is still visible today.

On the cultural side, the second half of the nineteenth century presented Florence with some interesting contradictions. In an atmosphere which was henceforth provincial and somewhat claustrophobic, a group of artists, imbued with a genuine spirit of renewal, created the Macchiaioli movement. Preceding the French Impressionists, Fattori, Signorini, Lega and the others who joined them are not considered to be the equals of Manet, Degas and Monet, but their influence on Italian painting was just as important.

Just as surprising is the issue of foreign "colonies". Florence, by this time, had little to offer other than her past, but her attraction was in no way diminished, and she drew numerous visitors who eventually decided to settle there. This success with foreigners also led to the creation of such important institutions as the Deutsche Kunsthistorisches Institut (1880), still one of the world's outstanding art history institutes. The Institut Français was founded in 1908, its British counterpart nine years later. The English even had their own romantic cemetery in the Piazza Donatello and held literary salons. Foreign collectors such as Stibbert and Horne created and financed museums which would bear their names. Robert Davidson wrote a *History of Florence* which would be definitive, as would Jacob

The light of dawn obscures the differences between ancient monuments and more modern structures. The square in front of the railway station and the Piazza dell' Unità, in the foreground, show the way that leads to the historic centre. In the square which separates Santa Maria Novella from the station, one has an idea of the creativity which has always marked urban development here. The station, a masterpiece of contemporary architecture dating from the 1930s, was designed by a group under the leadership of Giovanni Michelucci. Low and linear, and constructed of pink sandstone, it harmonises surprisingly well with the soaring, elegant Gothic apse of the church.

An imposing presence alongside the Autostrada del Sole (the motorway of the sun), the church of San Giovanni Battista is one of the rare aesthetically pleasing modern churches. Architect Giovanni Michelucci defined a church as follows: "The structural concept is simple... a tent supported by poles... The church is the way and the tent, the distance travelled and a temporary halt..." Thus, San Giovanni Battista would be a church for contemporary nomads.

Burckhardt's *Cicero* and *Architecture of Italian Renaissance*. In 1849 the Swiss G.P. Vieusseux founded the review *Antologia*, a literary office which today is one of the great Florentine institutions.

Italy's most important publishing houses, such as Olschki, Le Monnier, Sansoni and Barbera, came into being. Their publications were to mould generations of scholars. The nineteenth century's finest photographic and art reproduction business was set up by the Alinari brothers.

Florence was in the avant-garde of artistic and literary movements during the first decades of the twentieth century. Heated discussions about Futurism were to be heard at the Giubbe Rosse, a café in the Piazza Vittorio (today Piazza della Repubblica) amongst Ardengo Soffici, back from Paris in 1913, Giovanni Papini, Primo Conti and the founders of the movement from Milan. New reviews such as *La Voce*, *Il Marzocco* and *Lacerba*, then *Il Selvaggio* and *Solario*, formed the poles of contemporary thought which would dominate Italian culture for some fifty years. However, the morale and enterprising spirit of Florence seemed weakened, and the intellectual and artistic community seemed removed from the rest of Florence and unable to control the destiny of the city.

Two important projects stand out from the fascist period: Pier Luigi Nervi's municipal stadium, a bold, yet simple and rational, structure; and the Santa Maria Novella railway station, designed and constructed by the Gruppo Toscano whose leader, Giovanni Michelucci, was an internationally famous architect. The station is the same red as the stone of the apse of Santa Maria Novella, but its pure, simple lines holds their own against its neighbour, that masterpiece of Florentine Gothic.

The major figures of Italian prose and poetry were associated with the literary journals of the thirties and forties: Eugenio Montale, a future Nobel-prize winner; the poets Mario Luzi, Alfonso Gatto; Romano Bilenchi who, despite his youth, had written some of the most beautiful prose works of the twentieth century; Vasco Pratolini whose novels, full of humour, depict an authentic, "popular" Florence; Carlo Emilio Gadda, Tommaso Landolfi, Contini, Salvatore Quasimodo, Bonsanti and many more.

In painting, Rosai, with his evocations of the difficult life of the working class, the stones and plaster walls of a deserted city, brought the period preceding World War II to a close.

Towards the end of the War, the Resistance did not wait for the Allies to liberate the city. For the first time since it began its march northward, the Allied Command did not have to use force: the Tuscan Liberation Committee had already taken local affairs in hand. The first Allied troops were given a euphoric welcome, fascism was finished, bread was distributed and running water was restored.

Reconstruction began. The Florentines faced the difficulties of the post-war period — poverty and unemployment — with the hope of improving their living conditions. A great holiday took place the day the Gates of Paradise, which had been taken down and hidden, returned to the Baptistery. While restoring the doors, Bruno Bearzi, a master caster, had discovered that, under the bronze oxydation, Ghiberti's masterpiece was gilded. Bearzi thus restored the doors to their former splendour, and it was again evident why Michelangelo had dubbed them the Gates of Paradise.

Also reconstructed — with a few questionable architectural compromises — were the Por Santa Maria district as well as the route leading from the Porcellino to the Ponte Vecchio. The German consul, who dearly loved Florence, had tried to gain a peaceful German retreat and secure that Florence, like Rome, be declared an open city. But in vain: the German rear-guard blew up the route, along with all the bridges except for the Ponte Vecchio — which Hitler had crossed a few years earlier. The bridges have been rebuilt, and the Santa Trinità, Ammannati's engineering and architectural masterpiece, has been returned to its original form.

The city expanded quickly but not without the blemishes caused by cut-price building materials and projects of mediocre taste. The elegance of Arnolfo and Brunelleschi's creations did not seem to inspire architects or developers. We are far from the commitment of the great banking, merchant and noble families who were responsible for the grandeur of Florence because they believed in her past and her future. The Florentine suburbs are now as anonymous and undistinguished as those of any other city in any other country.

The Belvedere fortress, an imposing reminder of the grand-ducal period, forms a perfect triangle with the Pitti Palace and the Boboli Gardens. Built by Buontalenti in 1590 for Ferdinando I, the star-shaped fortifications crown the hill of San Giorgio and dominate the city. Their imposing character is tempered by the villa and its delightful porch through which one accedes to the enchantment of the surrounding hills. Today, the fortress is the site of important temporary exhibitions, devoted to sculptor Henry Moore, the painters of the Macchiaioli movement or the photographs of the Alinari Studio.

The Piazzale Michelangelo, today used as a car park for the innumerable sight-
seeing coaches, is one of the major examples of the transformations subjected on
Florence by Giuseppe Poggi in the last century. Even if "the results of the
romantic taste for vast perspectives and the urban panorama are incongruous
and alien to the characteristics of the city of Arnolfo di Cambio and
Brunelleschi" (Giovanni Fanelli, Firenze, 1980), the esplanade is one of the less
disastrous of the nineteenth-century innovations.

Immediately following the last war, the banks of the Arno were reconstructed. Period documents, plans and maps were closely consulted in an attempt to match the original style, prompting endless discussions over which criteria were to be observed. The final realisation was simply that there was a drastic need to provide lodgings or shops for those who had lost everything in the space of a few hours.

The squalid suburbs. Florence, like most other Italian cities, has not managed its modernisation with particular success, real estate speculation and the absence of serious urban planning being the culprits. This cityscape shows clearly the rupture of the old urban structure.

The Lungarno Vespucci and the Ponte Amerigo Vespucci which links the Borgo Ognissanti to the working class district of San Frediano. The bridge dates from the 1950s, while the embankment goes back to the mid-nineteenth century. One also sees a part of the Pescaia (barrage) di Santa Rosa which is shown on the earliest maps of Florence. Many years ago, when the Arno was clean and bathing not forbidden, children came here for a refreshing dip on hot summer days. Their favourite game consisted of standing on a ledge at the base of the waterfall and trying to remain upright under the cascade. This was their chance to enjoy the delights of a prolonged shower.

Another part of the elegant Lungarno Vespucci, with the Ponte alla Carraia, constructed after the war. At the corner of the Piazza Ognissanti, are situated two luxury hotels, the Grand Hotel and the Excelsior. They represent another aspect of the tourism to which the city owes its prosperity.

The Porta Romana (Roman Gate), constructed between 1328 and 1331 after plans by Jacopo Orcagna, is part of the last fortified wall that encircled Florence. It is linked on one side to the Boboli Gardens and, on the other, to the Belvedere Fortress and the Torrigiani Gardens. Here is the beginning of the Cassia, the old route to Siena and Rome. In the last few years, thanks to a working group from the University of Florence under the supervision of Francesco Bandini, efforts have been made to enhance what remains of the former ramparts. "The gates, the walls belong to the past, dead elements of the city. But one has merely to climb and walk along them, and they come back to life and belong to us, whereas otherwise, they are forgotten."(G. Michelucci, Su e gió per le antiche mura, Florence, 1983).In the centre of the piazza is a recent sculpture by Michelangelo Pistoletto.

A corner of the Piazza della Repubblica. The square was opened up as part of the "rehabilitation plan" of 1888, entailing the destruction of the Ghetto and the Old Market. Giovanni Fanelli deplored this as the "most serious real-estate error of the century".

The Café Gilli, Piazza della Repubblica, where other famous cafés such as Paskovsky and Donnini are located. This is also the site of the Giubbe Rosse, meeting-place of Florence's literary and artistic avant-garde since the beginning of the century, a period which witnessed the first confrontations — verbal and physical — between the Futurists of Marinetti and Soffici and the defenders of Classicism such as Papini and Prezzolini.

The residential area, between the historic centre and the suburbs, was constructed along the ring-road after the ramparts were razed in the last century. The Piazza d'Azeglio, a large tree-shaded square, rivalling those of Paris or London, is lined with elegant buildings housing both offices and flats.

Near the Piazza d'Azeglio stands the synagogue, built between 1872 and 1874 by the architects Treves and Micheli. Of oriental inspiration, this imposing structure, with its handsome verdigris dome, is one of the best examples of the architectural and decorative eclecticism of the nineteenth century.

The nineteenth century gave Florence her esplanades and avenues. Giuseppe Poggi's urban renewal project, realised between 1864 and 1877, radically changed the face of the city. This was the reaction, in 1873, of the eminent tourist Henry James: "I first knew Florence early enough, I am happy to say, to have heard the change for the worse, the taint of the modern order... Florence loses itself to-day in dusty boulevards and smart beaux quartiers...." However, the Piazza Beccaria, conceived as a halt along the way leading to the Viale dei Colli, "maintains a precise identity...almost metaphysical". (Laura Vinca Masini, Itinerari per Firenze, 1981). In the centre of the piazza is the Porta alla Croce.

93

The Piazza della Libertà, to the left, and the Piazza dell'Indipendenza, above,
both date from the vast upheavals of the last century. Facing the remains of the
old Porta San Gallo is the traditional triumphal arch, hastily constructed of poor
quality sandstone for the arrival of the first Lorraine grand duke, in 1739. In the
Piazza dell'Indipendenza statues of Bettino Ricasoli and Ubaldino Peruzzi
honour the Risorgimento.

Above: The Villa Vittoria, constructed in the last century. It originally housed one of the most important private collections of ancient art in Italy— that of the Contini-Bonaccossi family— now dispersed between heirs, the State and the National Gallery in Washington. Behind the villa is the the Centro Internazionale dei Congressi (International Convention Centre, part of which is underground), designed by Luigi Spadolini.

Opposite: The rear of the imposing Palazzo Capponi, dating from 1705, just a few steps from the S.S. Annunziata church.

In Florence, as in the rest of Italy, the terrace plays an essential role. The tall, narrow houses are dotted with these havens of peace tucked between staircases, behind chimneys, on tile roofs and in towers, providing privileged vantage points.

Pier Luigi Nervi's municipal stadium, constructed in 1932, is considered a remarkable example of the use of reinforced concrete. The dynamic design confers on any sporting event a sense of freedom and lightness.

*The race course is located in the centre of the Parco delle Cascine which is home to such diverse
public institutions as the School of Aerial Warfare, the University of Forest Sciences and the
Tennis Club of Florence. The Florentines have loved this park ever since it was opened by the
Grand Duke Piero Leopoldo for Ascension and certain other solemn occasions. Under the brief
Napoleonic occupation, the park became a public garden.*
Following pages: *The south-west suburbs. One can just detect the bell-tower and the dome of
the cathedral behind the hills to the right.*

THE OUTSKIRTS OF FLORENCE

The secondary roads which leave the city centre and climb towards the hills were, for the most part, built a long, long time ago. They were travelled on foot or on horseback, and even today, it is often necessary to abandon the car and continue on foot. The variety of perspectives is infinite, but certain elements remain fundamental: the soft, peaceful hills; a countryside completely remodelled by man yet remaining intact and natural: vineyards in their orderly rows, olive trees alternating with cypresses, houses and fields, villas and gardens, all organised in a perfect harmony.

Yet, never does the city let herself be forgotten: she is there, omnipresent, living, breathing, even if one turns one's back on her. Climb up to Santa Margherita a Montici, descend the hills of Fiesole by the Via Vecchia, arrive from Settignano at the Giardino (small garden) della Gamberaia at the Villa Capponi... these are but a few of the possible ways for the foreigner gradually to penetrate the secrets of Florence.

Florence would not be Florence without her hills. To understand their relationship, one must observe her in different lights, varying from season to season, day to day, hour to hour. Florence is also Fiesole, Bellosguardo, Settignano, Arcetri...there is no break between the culture, the tastes, the forms and the styles of the urban complex and the foothills, as vital and necessary as the city they have always surrounded and protected.

As long as five centuries ago, the chronicler Benedetto Dei observed that foreign travellers were frequently astounded by the hundreds of impressive structures located within a few miles' radius of the city: villas, castles, manors, monasteries, and gardens laid out according to geometric designs, the whole landscape manifesting a perfect harmony.

Florentine Renaissance and Humanism were actually expressed not only in the city's civil and religious architecture, in poetry and philisophical debate, in the splendour of the painting and the refinement of the decorative arts, but also in the way they modelled the surrounding countryside with an equal inspiration and success. Nature had to submit to man's rationale, while he, in carefully selecting the site of his dwelling place, sought to preserve its harmony. It was not mere coincidence that Leon Battista Alberti, author of the geometric façade of Santa Maria Novella and first great architectural theoretician of Renaissance, was also responsable for a definition of the rules to respect in the construction of sumptuous country houses and their integration with the environment. One understands the stupefaction of Ludovico Ariosto, author of *Orlando furioso*, upon observing the number of villas on the outskirts of Florence:

A veder pien di tante ville i colli
par che il terren ve le germogli...
(To see the hills dotted with so many villas,
one would believe they sprout from the earth...)

Beyond the villas and their gardens, the eye is drawn to the landscape: peasant houses, low stone walls bordering country roads, crops, and the eternal trio of vineyards (magnificent in summer, luxuriant in autumn), olive trees (being recultivated after recent devastating frosts) and cypresses (crowning the hills and taking on the lightness of the breeze).

What is the secret of this unique landscape? It all began between the end of the Middle Ages and the Renaissance, with the amassed wealth of the bankers and merchants. Florence grew, the guilds developed, and the large holdings of the Empire and Church were broken up. Merchants, artisans and professional people bought land to build their new country residences. The "master's house" or "casa da signore" was a place of refuge for the rich city dweller during the hot summer months. The fertile land around these houses was entrusted to the peasants who were no longer farmers but share-croppers, that is, associates of the master. He provided the capital, the peasant the raw labour. Harvests were divided in half, and the Florentine peasant thus gained a certain dignity, in the form of security and oral and material culture. This distinguished him almost until the present day, amazing travellers from foreign countries as well as

A taste for topiary (Ars topiaria) *is typical of most Florentine gardens, even the smaller, anonymous ones such as this.*

from other regions of Italy.

The "master's house", then, is the result of a city culture: its harmonious proportions and symmetry a reflection of the principles of Florentine architecture which had always been inspired by simple, well-proportioned models and light colours.

As the result of epidemics in the second half of the fourteenth century, and then the crises of the seventeenth, Florence and her environs became depopulated. The *signori* were forced to improve the conditions of their share-croppers, according them, among other things, a house. Often the master was even forced to turn over his own home so that the farmer would stay.

Today, as a result of emigration and mechanised farming, the rural population has dwindled, and many of these houses, converted, restored or sometimes disfigured, have once again become second homes for city dwellers. Dating from the Middle Ages, the Renaissance or the grand-ducal period, these beautiful country houses are characterised by their perfect proportions, their dovecotes, courtyards and windows that might be attributed to Alberti or Brunelleschi.

Aside from these houses, the hills are dotted with more imposing structures: villas which, in some cases, have been built on the remains of a mediaeval turreted castle, or a former *casa da signore*. The conversion work was often entrusted to experienced architects: Michelozzo, for example, worked on the Medici villas at Cafaggiolo and Fiesole, Giuliano da Sangallo the splendid villa at Poggio a Caiano, and Buontalenti the Grand Duke Ferdinando I's residence at Artiminio. In general, however, little is known of the creators of these splendid homes. But it is obvious that they were constructed with as much loving attention as were the palaces in town — if not more. Here, the ensemble could be completed and enhanced by geometrically designed gardens, based on Classical Roman models and demonstrating a thorough knowledge of topiary.

A garden of delights, a place for philosophical meditation or a gathering place for literary discussions, the most beautiful Medici villas

The Villa Barone at Montemurlo, to the north-west of Florence, was, in the sixteenth century, a large estate belonging to the Tempi family. It features in the "vedute" of Florence and Tuscany executed by Zocchi in the eighteenth century.

welcomed the greatest Humanist minds of the day: Marsilio Ficino, Pico della Mirandola, Agnolo Poliziano, Lorenzo the Magnificent, to name but a few. Surrounded by ornamental orchards and groves of lemon trees, the villa was an expression of the rebirth of Florentine civilisation and of the scientific studies devoted to agriculture at the city's Accademia dei Geofili from the time of the Medicis up until the Lorraine reforms. The villa, often with a farm, fitted in perfectly with its rural surroundings, fields, rows of cypresses, the silvery olive trees, the holm-oaks, the laurel and the boxwood of classical secret gardens.

Unfortunately, some of these estates lost their character as a result of the excessive restorations of the romantic era. The garden *all'italiana* was replaced by the English park; meanwhile houses were redecorated or even reconstructed. Designers continued to seek inspiration in the Middle Ages or the Renaissance, but it was merely to create an eclectic reconstitution in which Classical simplicity was unknown — or undesired.

From this period, foreigners began to take a passionate interest in Florence and her hills. Travellers often arrived in Florence as pilgrims and settled there permanently. The pilgrimage was uninterrupted: from Jane Austen to Henry James and D.H. Lawrence, from Stibbert to Sir John Temple who would restore, recreate or invent a number of notable houses in the hills of Fiesole, including the famous mock-mediaeval Vincigliata Castle. We must not forget Bernard Berenson, the great specialist of Italian Renaissance art and Sienese painting, who arrived in Italy at the end of the last century and lived for many decades at the Villa I Tatti. Having enriched American museums with his discoveries, he bequeathed his villa, along with an extensive library and an extraordinary collection of paintings, to Harvard University.

Thus was born, on the slopes of San Domenico, Settignano, Fiesole, Bellosguardo and, later on, along the hill-route (the Viale dei Colli), a cultured and cosmopolitan society which had chosen to adopt Florence and her environs as an indispensable setting for their intellectual pursuits and artistic inspiration.

La Petraia was originally a mediaeval fortified ensemble comprising manor house, peasant dwellings and craft workshops. Buontalenti converted it into a sumptuous villa for the Medicis, and the land was attached to the property they already held at Castello. The garden, formerly considered one of the finest examples of Florentine landscaping (despite the modifications all'inglese *in the last century), no longer boasts the "grandiose upkeep which was the case when Just Utens painted it in 1599". (G. Lensi Orlandi,* Le ville di Firenze di qua d'Arno, *1954) La Petraia now belongs to the State and is open to visitors. It has suffered from the many changes of style inflicted by its various inhabitants, including King Vittorio Emmanuele II.*

"A stunning introduction of the Florentine Romanesque into the purest Tuscan countryside", San Miniato al Monte with its green and white marble decoration remains a place of calm and contemplation. With the Baptistery and the Badia Fiesolina, it is among the finest examples of this style so different from the Lombard Romanesque.

A stroll along Viale dei Colli (Avenue of the Hills) comes to a glorious end at San Miniato. The Viale and its staircases were created by Giuseppe Poggi. The Palazzo dei Vescovi (Bishop's Palace), to the right, dates from 1295.

Poggi's staircase leads to the Cimitero Monumentale delle Porte Sante (Monumental Cemetery of the Holy Gates), a curious example of the funerary eclecticism of the previous century. The cemetery, surrounded by cypresses, has a certain melancholy charm.

During the siege of 1350, Michelangelo transformed this sixteenth century tower into an artillery outpost. The assailants tried to level the tower but in vain: Michelangelo had fortified it with woollen mattresses and bales of cotton .

The hill of Bellosguardo is, without a doubt, the most beloved by men of letters, regardless of nationality — Galileo, Foscolo or Henry James, for example. The area being off the tourist trail, this villa is practically a secret. In the foreground is the tower of Bellosguardo, the former home of the family of Guido Cavalcanti, a friend of Dante. Later, Oscar Wilde was a guest here. The garden and the rooms provide a marvellous view of Florence melting gently into the hills behind her. Next door is the famous Villa dell' Ombrellino, where one can experience the wonderful charm of the tower. Unfortunately, the rest has been closed to the public, since, after years of meticulous restoration, the owner Baron Franchetti has converted it into a hotel.

Here we are in the heart of ancient Fiesole, originally an Etruscan settlement, then Roman. From the bell-tower of the cathedral, one overlooks the Roman amphitheatre, one of the oldest in the world, and the baths with their arcades. This magic spot is imbued with grandeur and history. The stones of ancient Fiesole were used during the Middle Ages in the construction of numerous churches and convents, and only when excavations began, at the end of the eighteenth century, were these ruins brought to light.

A splendid Florentine villa in the midst of its park: a haven of peace and greenery.

Casa da Signore owes its name to its mediaeval tower. These country homes built by rich
Florentines in the fourteenth century were often subsequently inhabited by peasants. Nowadays,
returned to their original purpose, they serve as weekend or holiday homes for the bourgeoisie.
The quality of restoration is frequently debatable.

La Lastra, on the road to Bologna. Beyond the entrance courtyard, the woods of holm-oak and the greenhouses, one discovers this thirteenth century palace which was transformed in the fifteenth century into a sumptuous villa. Happily, the renovations of the last century did not mar the nobility of the structure. Jacopo Salviati, whose family had owned the property since the fifteenth century, abandoned it on New Year's Day in 1638, when his wife presented him with a basket containing the head of his young lover wrapped in an embroidered nightgown.

One can visit the gardens of the Villa Schifanoia, today the seat of Rosary College, by contacting "Agriturist", an organisation which arranges farmhouse holidays in the region.

In 1348, with the plague decimating Florence, Giovanni Boccaccio retreated to the Villa Palmieri amidst a group of fun-loving, carefree friends. Unfortunately, the villa has not retained its original appearance. It has been transformed on many occasions, as has the garden with, in 1697, the planting of lemon trees and later "Romantic" modifications. At the turn of the century, it belonged to Lord Crawford. Queen Victoria, who like her wealthier subjects, loved to come and sample the heady charms of Florence, was a guest here on two occasions.

Right: *While strolling in the Florentine countryside, one often comes across villas such as this one, its simple elegance enhanced by its Italian-style garden.*

The Torre del Gallo (far left) is a fake. At the beginning of the nineteenth century, an antique dealer named Bardini, following the fashion of the time, built on top of the mediaeval remains to create a display area for his collections of art works and furniture. This marvellous spot, in the midst of the hills, is just a few minutes from Florence via Poggio Imperiale, Arcetri (where Galileo's house and astronomical observatory are located) and Santa Margherita a Montici, dating from the fourteenth century. Along the way are dozens of villas such as the Villa Capponi whose exterior is an example of pure Renaissance style. The whole countryside is criss-crossed by paths and narrow roads, punctuated by little churches such as the one shown to the left.

The cloister of the Certosa del Galluzzo displays the splendour of its geometric volumes. This Carthusian monastery now houses a centre for the restoration of old books, founded after the 1966 flood when all damaged volumes were gathered here. One must not leave the monastery without visiting the magnificent chemist's shop where medicinal herbal liqueurs made by the monks are still sold.

Part of the Chiostro Grande (large cloister), once graced by the lunettes painted by Pontormo, who sought refuge here from the plague of 1523. Faded and practically illegible, the frescoes are now conserved in the museum of the Palazzo degli Studi.

An overview of the Certosa, perched atop a hill and surrounded by olive trees. From above, one grasps its scale and balance. This imposing edifice dates from between the fourteenth and sixteenth centuries from about the time when the church of San Lorenzo was built.

*Taking the Via Pistoiense,
one soon arrives at
Artimino, a mediaeval
village of Etruscan origin,
with houses looking onto
the large square.*

A panoramic view of this evocative, unspoilt village. The Romanesque parish church of Santa Maria e San Leonardo is mentioned as far back as the year 998. Recent restoration and research has confirmed that Etruscan cinerary urns and other materials were used in its construction.

Another historic Medici villa, built between 1539 and 1594 by Buontalenti for the Grand Duke Ferdinando I. Located within what was once Cosimo I's vast hunting preserve near Poggio a Caiano, the Villa di Artimino is reminiscent of fortified architecture, but its many chimneys confer a certain playfulness. Utens' famous lunettes with bird's-eye views of the Medici villas, used to be exhibited here; they are now housed in the Firenze com'era museum.

Above: *The imposing Castello dell'Imperatore (Emperor's Castle), built for Federico II in 1248; next to it is the Renaissance basilica, a masterpiece by Giuliano da Sangallo.*

Right: *The suburbs now extend so far that one might be led to believe that Florence and Prato form a single entity. This would be an error, since Prato (whose centre is shown here) has always managed to maintain a noble independence from the Republic of Florence, even though it was incorporated as of 1351. Boasting ancient origins — Ligurian, Etruscan and eventually, Roman — the city became a cultural and artistic centre while developing its textile industry.*

Sunlight dapples houses and a crenellated castle evoking a faraway past and a way of life which no longer belong to this place.

Houses and hamlets scattered through the hills around Prato. Here, nature is rugged and untamed but she seems protective rather than threatening.

Built in 1227, the Ponte alle Grazie resisted the onslaught of the flood of 1333, which claimed the Ponte Vecchio and the Ponte alla Carraia. Photographs dating from the first half of the nineteenth century show the tiny houses (inhabited by nuns from 1370 to 1424) still perched on the bridge. It did not, however, escape the German mines of August 1944.

FURTHER READING

LITERATURE

Boccaccio, *Giovanni*, Decameron, *Dent, 1970.*
Forster, *E. M.*, Room with a View, *Penguin, 1969.*
Goethe, *Johann Wolfgang von*, Italian Journey 1786-88, *Penguin, 1970.*
James, *Henry*, Italian Hours, *Ecco Press, 1988.*
Lawrence, *D. H.*, Etruscan Places, *Olive Press, 1986.*
McCarthy, *Mary*, Stones of Florence, *Heinemann, 1959.*
Wilkins, *E. H.*, History of Italian Literature, *Harvard University Press, 1975.*

ART

Antal, *Frederick*, Florentine Painting and its Social Background, *Harvard University Press, 1987.*
Anthony, *E.W.*, Early Florentine Architecture and Decoration, *Hacker Art Books, 1975.*
Avery, *Charles*, Florentine Renaissance Sculpture, *John Murray, 1970.*
Berenson, *Bernard*, Drawings of the Florentine Painters, *Greenwood Press, 1938.*
Burckhardt, *Jacob*, Architecture of the Italian Renaissance, *Penguin, 1987.*
Cellini, *Benvenuto*, Autobiography, *Phaidon, 1983*
Cirker, *Hayward*, Italian Master Drawings from the Uffizi, *Dover Publications, 1984.*
Cole, *Bruce*, Italian Art, 1250-1550: Relation of Renaissance Art to Life and Society, *Harper & Row, 1987.*
Hartt, *Frederick*, History of Italian Renaissance Art, *Thames & Hudson, 1988.*
Turner, *Nicholas*, Florentine Drawings of the Sixteenth Century, *British Museum Publications, 1986.*
Varriano, *John L.*, Italian Baroque and Roccoco Architecture, *Oxford University Press, 1986.*
Vasari, *Giorgio*, Lives of the Most Eminent Painters, Sculptors and Architects, *Medici, 1959.*
Whelpton, *Barbara*, Painters' Florence, *Johnson Publications, 1971.*

GUIDES

Baedecker, Florence, *Automobile Association, 1984.*
Chaney, *Edward, & Acton, Harold*, Florence: A Traveller's Companion, *Constable, 1986.*
Cultural Guides, Florence and Tuscany, *Phaidon, 1986.*
Fodor, Florence and Venice, *Hodder & Stoughton, 1987.*
Kent, *John*, Florence and Siena, *Viking, 1989.*
Monmarche, *François*, Florence, *Times Books, 1987.*
Scott, *Rupert*, Florence Explored, *Bodley Head, 1987.*
Stace, *Christopher*, City of the Lily, *Dent, 1989.*

HISTORY

Brucker, *Gene A.*, Love and Marriage in Renaissance Florence, *Weidenfeld & Nicolson, 1986.*
Brucker, *Gene A.*, Renaissance Florence, *University of California Press, 1983.*
Carmichael, *Ann G.*, Plague and the Poor in Early Renaissance Florence, *Cambridge University Press, 1986.*
Cochrane, *Eric W.*, Florence in the Forgotten Centuries 1527-1800 : A History of Florence and the Florentines in the Age of the Grand Dukes, *University of Chicago Press, 1976*
Compagni, *Dino*, Chronicle of Florence, *University of Pennsylvania Press, 1986.*
Coppa, *Frank J.*, Dictionary of Modern Italian History, *Greenwood Press, 1985.*
Hale, *John R.*, Florence and the Medici : Patterns of Control, *Thames and Hudson, 1983.*
Machiavelli, *Niccolo*, Literary Works of Machiavelli, *Greenwood Press, 1979.*
Machiavelli, *Niccolo*, The Prince and Other Political Writings, *Dent, 1983.*
Stephens, *J.N.*, Fall of the Florentine Republic 1512-30, *Oxford University Press, 1983.*

*The dome of San Lorenzo with, in the foreground,
the Medici tombs.*

Acknowledgements

The publisher and Guido Rossi, the
photographer, would like to thank air force SMA
2 Reparto and, in particular, Marechalo Di Chiara,
for their help. They would also like to thank the
pilots of Jet A1, Enrico Biseni and Carlo Pini. All
photography was authorised under statute SMA
no. 733 of 14 July 1989.

The author of the text expresses his gratitude to
Giovanna Bergamaschi, Mariarosa Schiaffino and
Alberto Conforti of Idealibri and to Philippe
Marchand of Editions Didier Millet for their
contribution to the conception and editing
of this work.